# We Have Fun Together

by Linda Lott  illustrated by Francesca Carabelli

**Target Skill** Character and Setting

**Scott Foresman**
is an imprint of

Here is Red.

Red likes to peck.

Here is Red.

Peck! Peck! Peck!

Here is Legs.

Legs likes to hop.

Here is Legs.

Hop! Hop! Hop!

Red pecks on logs.

Legs hops on a leg.

Red can peck.

Legs can do a jig.

The pals have fun!